CW01652729

# First Steps to FENG SHUI

Hermann von Essen

ISBN: 1 86476 090 7



This edition for
SELECT EDITIONS
Devizes
Wiltshire, UK

The photographic images used on pages 12 and 40, in this book, were obtained from IMSI's MasterClips Collection, 75 Rowland Way, Novato, CA 94945, USA.

A basic Feng Shui principle

*your*
**house**
reflects your life

*your*
**life**
reflects your house.

Both go hand in hand!

# Contents

page

# What is "Feng Shui"?

## Living in harmony with our environment

Feng Shui can be seen as the "art & science of living in harmony with our environment". This can be achieved by combining two approaches:

- Tuning our environment to meet our needs
- Tuning ourselves, gaining understanding and refining behaviour to relate better to our existing environment.

Feng Shui works with the energies which surround us. It can be practiced without relating to any religion or superstition.

## Understanding the continuous energy exchange

Feng Shui describes the continuous interaction between ourselves and our environment. We promote good Feng Shui in areas where we spend most of our time: the home (including the garden) and the workplace (for some people even their car).

Fresh flowers bring abundance and ch'i into our life.

With thankful acknowledgement to Gena Hamilton for editing this book.

## Feng Shui

We experience an energy feedback from our immediate environment, which we have usually created ourselves. If it is harmonious, balanced and connected to natural daylight and nature, the energies uplift us. However, if it is dark, dirty and filled with clutter, it will depress us and hold back our progress. The choice is ours and Feng Shui is our guide to improvement!

Naturally, there is also an energy exchange with the people who surround us regularly. Partners, family members, work colleagues, co-students, peers, etc, all contribute to how we feel. Feng Shui can offer compatibility insights and relationship remedies even in that area.

### Effect on health, wealth and success

A home with good Feng Shui will contribute to health, wealth, balance and harmony. Visitors will feel welcome and at ease, intruders repelled. Feng Shui can even achieve turning a "good house" into a better one. A business with good Feng Shui will contribute to the success and prosperity of the enterprise. Customers are intuitively attracted to deal with such businesses and feel confident and comfortable doing so.

Modern Feng Shui can accommodate western lifestyles and conditions. In the hands of an experienced practitioner it is applied effectively in both hemispheres, provided some correct adjustments are made for Southern Hemisphere conditions where applicable.

Most Feng Shui books presently on the market relate to the northern hemisphere or describe "authentic Feng Shui", which was developed in China in ancient times,when there was no awareness of the southern hemisphere. Since then, Feng Shui has expanded into the world. Conditions vary between the hemispheres and some Feng Shui topics are affected, while others remain unchanged. This publication has been written for use in the Northern and Southern Hemispheres. The reader chooses the appropriate version.

## The ancient "Art & Science", called "Feng Shui"

### Pronunciation

First, let us look at the confusing pronunciation of Feng Shui, represented by the two illustrated Chinese characters, meaning "wind" and "water". The English spelling is "Feng Shui" but we say: "Fung Shway" ("Fung" rhymes with the word "tongue"). Another important and frequently used word is "Ch'i", also written as: "Q'i" and pronounced "Chee".

### Presentation of Feng Shui

Although ancient and traditional Feng Shui may present in an archaic or typically oriental way, the essence of the teaching can often be explained by understanding basic energy flow.

Here is an example of a topic presented in symbolism: the "coffin position", relating to a bed position with the foot end towards the door. The legend says: "this is how one will be carried out after death: feet first." However, the reasoning behind it is pure energy control. It is undesirable ch'i-flow entering the door hits the bed directly as this causes unrest and insomnia. It is preferable ch'i has a chance to meander through the room first and then nurture the sleeping person. (Note: ch'i = life-force, as explained in further chapters) This book shows that, with an understanding of the principles, Feng Shui can effectively be applied to modern times, serving various life-styles and both hemispheres.

## Feng Shui

### A brief History

Feng Shui was practiced in China well before 2000 BC. Two basic concepts emerged, known as the "Form School" and the "Compass School". These main streams are usually included in today's modern Feng Shui applications.

The Form School (also named Landscape School)was guided by Lao-Tse, originator of a widespread philosophy known as "Taoism". This school developed in a southern province of China, characterised by an impressive landscape of dramatic mountains, steep hills and sweeping rivers. Evidently, this Feng Shui topic relates to the "form" of the landscape and other physical features surrounding our environment. These principles apply around the house as well as internally in every room through the logical application of the "Celestial animals" theory.

The Compass School was guided by Con-Fu-Tse, known in the west as "Confucius". It emerged in flat country and therefore related to compass orientations because there were no other features to refer to. Through the Chinese Magic Square (the "Lo Shu" grid, said to be found on the shell of a tortoise) the science of Chinese numerology was developed with a link to the famous "Book of Changes", named the "I Ching". The "Former heaven sequence ba-gua" and the "Later heaven sequence ba-gua", the eight trigrams and the sixty-four hexagrams are all included in the Compass School and influence today's Feng Shui around the world.

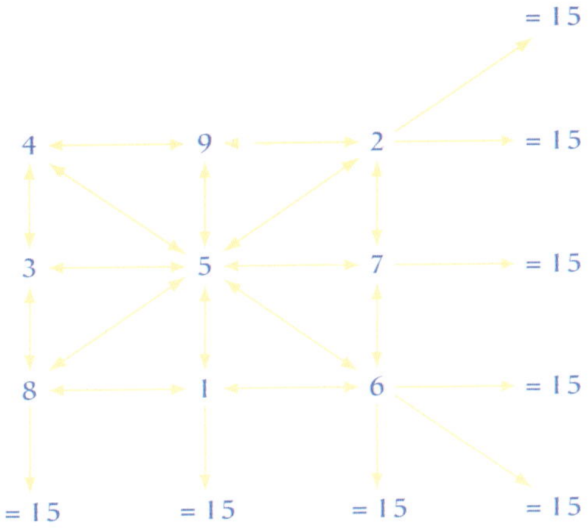


The Chinese Magic Square (Lo-Shu grid) as found on the shell of a tortoise.

The more modern Black Hat School is a derivative of the Compass school, using the same ba-gua principles but independent of compass directions. The most used entrance to the house is logically lined up with the "K'an" (water) trigram of the ba-gua, symbolising "flow" and "career path". Other areas of the house, such as the "prosperity corner" or "relationships corner" are then positioned in relation to the entrance.

## Hemisphere sensitivity

Although there are many Feng Shui books on the market, few other titles address the specific differences associated with the conditions of the southern hemisphere.
Although many theories are valid, some directional and orientational aspects require adjustment for the southern hemisphere. It is no surprise that to many Australian and New Zealand readers the Feng Shui books for the northern hemisphere create confusion. A simple illustration: in the moderate climates of southern hemisphere countries, the cold comes from the south and not from the North, as most books try to tell us.

## "Ch'i", the essential life-force

### Introduction

Avoiding staleness in a corner promotes good ch'i flow

"Ch'i" and ch'i-control are the most important aspects of Feng Shui. "Ch'i" is sometimes written as "Q'i" but both are pronounced "chee". The Japanese call it "K'i" and in India it is known as "Prana". Although the importance of ch'i is readily known and accepted in oriental and holistic thinking, most people in western society have been brought up believing life can be sustained sufficiently by food, water and the air we breathe. Ch'i, however, is essential to our vitality and it keeps us connected to the earth.

### Qualities of ch'i

Feng Shui works with different qualities of ch'i. For a basic understanding and to remain within the scope of this publication, these have been condensed into three main categories:

- sheng ch'i (naturally flowing and nurturing)
- sha(r) ch'i (straight lined, becoming destructive)
- si ch'i (trapped, becoming toxic)

Sheng ch'i is natural ch'i, available in abundance at the earth's surface. It meanders gently through the landscape. Naturally, it is easier to tap into it in nature than when surrounded by concrete and steel.

Sha ch'i is created by man-made channelling of original sheng-ch'i into a straight line, e.g. in long streets (outside) or long corridors (inside). Once forced into a straight line, ch'i accelerates and becomes aggressive and destructive.

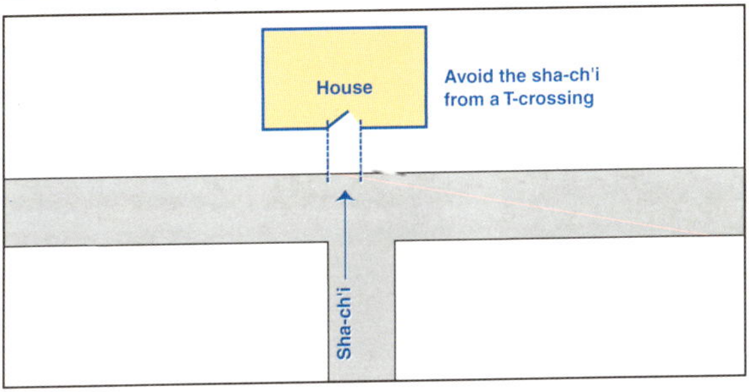


An example of sha-ch'i

Si ch'i is present when ch'i is trapped and eventually its vitality expires, becoming toxic and affecting our health.

### Examples of beneficial ch'i

natural ch'i
(undisturbed nature)

meandering ch'i
(normal human activity)

waving ch'i
(water environment)

### Examples of damaging ch'i

sha ch'i
(destructive)

turbulent ch'i
(too much human activity)

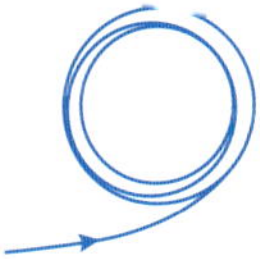

si-ch'i
(trapped and toxic)

Some images of ch'i, as it can flow in nature or inside a house.

## Assessing ch'i

Gently flowing water promotes prosperity and a good chi-flow

Ch'i-flow can be traced by dowsing, a useful way to assess the ch'i-connection of any building. Ch'i-analysis, prior to and after a Feng Shui audit, is used to confirm that ch'i-flow related Feng Shui improvements have been implemented properly. The art of dowsing includes the use of a dowsing rod or pendulum to trace energies.

## Ch'i and health

A person who is able to connect with sheng-ch'i regularly will feel healthy and vibrant. The immune system will usually be strong and colds and flu are a rarity. It is a matter of having sheng-ch'i available in those places where we spend most of our time. The bedroom has a high priority as, on average, a third of our life span is spent there. Next is the house in general and then the workplace. Ideally, all these places are nurtured by sheng- ch'i. If they are lacking a good ch'i-connection, we can usually improve the situation with Feng Shui.

Connecting with nature enhances personal ch'i

## Ch'i connection

"Needing a break" on a recurring basis usually indicates a poor link with sheng-ch'i. Alternatively, benefits of ch'i may be destroyed by "riding on stress". Spending considerable time inside houses or workplaces with a lack of ch'i depletes our vitality and eventually our immune system. The same is experienced in areas with high EMR (electro-magnetic radiation) or a surplus of positive ionised air, a common modern day pollutant caused by computer monitors, TVs, air conditioners, nylon carpet, etc.

## Ch'i and lifestyle

A person needing a holiday every half year "to get away from it all" usually maintains an unhealthy life-style.

During the first week of the holiday, it is more than likely that a health crisis occurs as the body goes into shock. After acclimatisation and recovery during the second week, it is time to pack the suitcases, return home and the cycle is repeated.

## Ch'i and the house

Theoretically, living in a healthy house enables us to stay there for the rest of our life and remain healthy. It may not be very exciting but it is effective. Why not combine the best of two worlds: have a healthy house and also enjoy a healthy holiday. Not for "survival purposes", but just for the sheer joy of having fun and experiencing different places and cultures.

## Back to nature

An unhealthy lifestyle, possibly because of a job commitment, can be compensated by regularly connecting with nature, as in walking, bicycling or participation in non-competitive sports. Car and TV recreation are counter-productive to connecting with nature.

Maintaining good health requires ch'i-awareness and common sense.

Nature supporting ch'i.

## Ch'i-Flow In House And Garden

### Good ch'i starts with the garden

The garden supports the house and is an integral part of the Feng Shui of a property. The garden relays sheng-ch'i from nature to the house and filters out possible sha-ch'i. Avoid tall trees close to the house and never allow branches touch or overhang the roof. The advantages are:

- Ch'i-flow and daylight can enter the house without obstruction
- Trees drop fewer leaves into the gutters
- Branches do not thrash noisily on the roof during storms
- Trees are at a safe distance from the house, hence roots cannot damage the foundations.

Restrict plants near the house to very low shrubs or flower beds. Alternatively, the house can be bordered by a lawn or paved area, but preferably not by concrete. The further the distance from the house, the higher the vegetation can be. The result of this approach resembles amphitheatre style. The depth of the amphitheatre can be short on the black tortoise side of the house, but needs to be long on the red phoenix side (see "Celestial animals" chapter).

### Invite ch'i in

Natural sheng-ch'i continues to flow inside if we make it "feel at home". It needs to find our main entrance easily. We can understand the behavioural properties of ch'i energy by imagining ch'i to be a "foreign visitor" who needs to be invited. We can facilitate this as follows:

- We ensure our property attracts sheng ch'i. A good garden design presents an inviting front gate, displaying a quality house number or name.
- Next, we provide a clear and inviting path from the front gate to the main entrance of the house. The shape of the driveway, paths, borderlines and vegetation co-operate to guide us. Gently flowing paths without obstacles achieve

the best results. Cracked concrete, uneven steps, garbage bins, clutter, weeds and litter inhibit the flow. We also avoid plants with spiky leaves or thorns along the entry path.

- We avoid ch'i-flow being obstructed by a large tree or post close to the main entrance.
- We ensure the main entrance of the house is clearly identified. Some houses present a puzzle by having all doors blinded by flyscreens or security doors, all looking the same. The lack of a doorbell or doorknocker may add to the confusion.

A long corridor with a strategically placed plant for meandering ch'i flow.

Once inside, ch'i must not be repelled by mirrors or converted into sha-ch'i by leading it into a long straight corridor. An internal landscape formed by the layout of the floor plan and the placement of furniture preferably allows the ch'i to maintain its own meandering character.

Tuning an entrance to attract ch'i.

## Ch'i –flow paths

Ch'i usually enters through an active door. It rarely enters through a door which is never used. Ch'i may leave by another door (provided the house has more than two outside doors). The inflow and outflow and the route through the house can be easily detected by dowsing. (For more information, contact the author or a local dowsers society). The ideal situation is obtained when ch'i visits every room and meanders gently, covering every area and corner. It is essential that ch'i also finds an exit to avoid accumulation of stagnant si-ch'i.

## Floor plans and furnishings

Features to avoid:

- A long straight corridor
- A front and back door in line with each other
- Two internal doors opposite each other
- Rooms with windows in opposite walls
- Rooms with fewer than two solid walls (i.e. walls without a door, passage or window)
- Narrow cavities between furniture or between furniture and a corner
- A staircase starting immediately behind the main entrance
- Bad smells (stale air, dampness, chemicals, solvents)
- Concentrations of EMR (electro-magnetic radiation)
- Energy tension from geopathic stress
- The use of artificial materials, such as: concrete (including concrete tiles, blocks, etc.), nylon carpet, PVC, Lino and other plastics, artificial plants and flowers, etc.
- Lack of daylight (every room needs at least one window)
- Fluoro lighting (emits toxic 50Hz frequency)
- Iron and steel objects (these attract EMR)
- Loud noise levels
- Clutter in any form
- Offending mirror positions (see next chapter)

## Ch'i-Flow And Mirrors

### Features to promote:

- Plenty of natural daylight (open curtains and blinds fully, curtain rods need to extend on both sides to open curtains fully aside from the window, repair fatigued roller blinds)
- Consider skylights in areas with a lack of daylight (but not directly above a bed or seating)
- Use natural materials, such as wooden floorboards, woollen carpet, cotton, linen, cork, ceramic or terracotta tiles, clay bricks, living plants, fresh flowers, etc.

### The feeling of good ch'i

Some houses "feel good", others "feel unpleasant". This can even change from room to room. Although these experiences may be difficult to explain, there is often a link with the quality and abundance of ch'i. A house with a good ch'i-flow attracts welcome visitors and communication is easy and pleasant. Such a house is usually easier to sell when placed on the market. A house with an unbalanced ch'i-flow can be very difficult to sell, despite repainting or recarpeting. A Feng Shui analysis prior to selling a house is usually a good investment.

The choice of colour defines this entrance as a typical back door.

## Ch'i-Flow And Mirrors

### Behavioural patterns of ch'i

Although it is difficult to define ch'i we can understand some of its behavioural properties:

- Ch'i can travel with the wind, although fierce winds disperse it
- Ch'i loses its vitality in stale areas or when it is trapped
- Ch'i is encouraged by natural daylight and discouraged by darkness
- Ch'i can be retained by water, although stagnant water induces staleness
- Ch'i is reflected by mirrors in a similar way as visible light

### Mirrors repel ch'i

Since mirrors repel ch'i, we must not position a mirror opposite:

- doors (this will send the ch'i back)
- windows (this causes a ch'i-draught, inducing unrest)
- passages (this will force one-way ch'i instead of allowing it to find its own way)
- other mirrors (this causes reverberation, inducing unrest)
- beds (the body cannot dispose of its own waste-ch'i during sleep, which eventually may lead to the development of chronic medical conditions)

A mirror inside a room opposite the door prevents the ch'i from entering and we create a "dead room". However, a mirror outside a room opposite the door allows the ch'i to enter but not to leave. It becomes trapped, leading to the very unhealthy and stagnant si-ch'i.

## Feng Shui

Be aware that a glass-framed picture may work as a mirror under certain light conditions. Consider the use of reflection-free glass or replace it by an oil painting or block-mounted print.

### Other aspects of mirrors

- Apply mirrors sparingly. A bedroom full of mirrors can become a "horror-chamber" in relation to restful and healthy sleep.
- Larger surfaces, composed of mirror tiles, break up and scatter any reflected image.
- Two mirrors meeting each other in a corner have a surprising effect. Wherever we stand, our image splits in half with a line running vertically through the centre of the body.
- We need to position a mirror allowing the tallest person in the house a full image of the face, without the forehead being cut off.

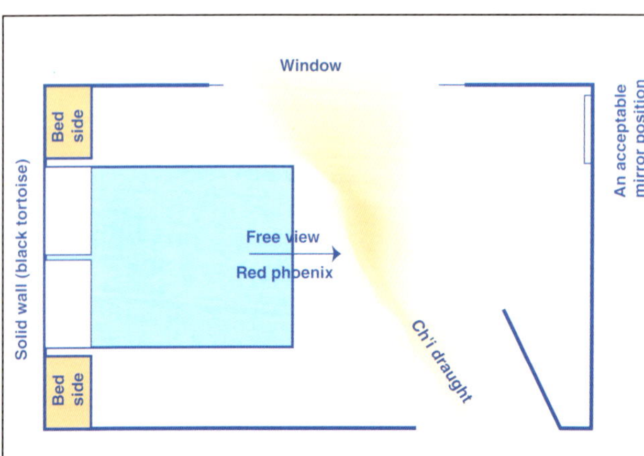


An example of a balanced and healthy bedroom

## Yin & Yang

### Yin and yang principles

Yin and yang are the two opposite forces which influence all aspects of life, nature and existence. They oppose and join each other, they love and hate each other, they continuously interact and they represent the duality in life. We assign many different attributes to yin and yang, depending on the circumstances. The most common ones are:

| Yang | Yin |
|---|---|
| Male | Female |
| Positive | Negative |
| Active | Passive |
| Day | Night |
| Light | Dark |
| Summer | Winter |
| Hot | Cold |
| Sun | Moon |
| Dynamic | Static |
| Sweet | Sour |
| Fire | Water |
| etc, | |

## Feng Shui

This is the well-known "Tai-ch'i" symbol that expresses the never-ending energy exchange between yin and yang. The two shapes oppose, embrace and chase each other and always complement each other.

Yin and yang embracing and chasing each other at the same time.

Yin and yang can also be represented by lines.

A yang line shows a solid uninterrupted line.

A yin line shows a small gap in the centre.

### Yin and yang applications

Yin and yang lines are used to build trigrams (consisting of three lines) and hexagrams (consisting of six lines). The eight possible trigrams are used to build a ba-gua (see following pages). The sixty-four possible hexagrams are attached to the sixty-four chapters of the "I Ching", book of changes.

### Yin and yang balance

Feng Shui promotes balance between the representations of yin and yang in houses, gardens, rooms, etc. A balanced place feels good while one which is seriously out of balance may feel uninviting or even repelling. We also try to maintain the yin / yang balance in our daily behaviour and in all aspects of life, sometimes intuitively, sometimes by reasoning. Disturbance of this balance often leads to discomfort, mischief or conflict.

## Trigrams

### Building a trigram

Combining the duality of yin and yang three times gives us 2 to the power of 3, which equals 8 possible combinations as follows:

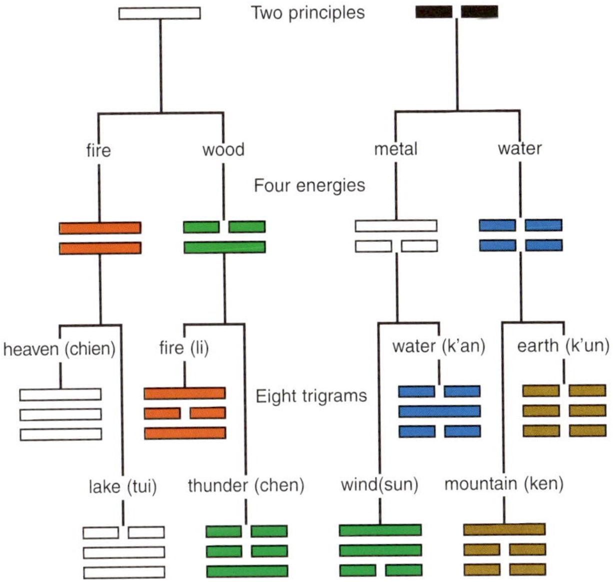


Since a trigram has an odd number of lines, there is never equilibrium between yin and yang within a trigram. There is always a resulting force.

### Building a ba-gua

When we place all eight trigrams in a circle, or rather in an octagon, we obtain a "ba-gua". Depending on the sequence of the trigrams we achieve a perfect balance of forces (static ba-gua) or an active exchange of forces (dynamic ba-gua). Traditionally, trigrams have been arranged in two sequences: the "former heaven sequence" (static) and "later heaven sequence" (dynamic).

## The Forces of the Ba-gua

### Former heaven sequence

The former heaven sequence is based on the position of the planets, therefore only one version is valid for both hemispheres. The specific properties of this sequence express total balance, peace and tranquillity. Every trigram is the inverted image of its opposing trigram: a yin line on one side of the ba-gua mirrors a yang line on the opposite side and vice versa.

The application areas of this static ba-gua are:

- The "ba-gua mirror", a powerful "Ch'i-control device", usually printed in red, green and gold with a circular mirror in the centre. It is obtainable from Chinese shops, usually in three different sizes. The ba-gua mirror draws sheng-ch'i inwards and repels sha-ch'i and therefore can be hung outside above an entrance. However, if a house has more than one entrance, it must only be hung above the ch'i-entry and never above a ch'i-exit. Within a house it should only be used on recommendation of an experienced Feng Shui practitioner as it can upset a proper ch'i-flow and may do more harm than good.

The ba-gua mirror in the "former heaven sequence"

- The layout and positioning of **grave sites and matters dealing with the past**. This is a highly respected Feng Shui topic in eastern countries, where it is given a high priority. The western world gives it less importance and it is outside the scope of this publication.

When comparing several ba-gua mirrors, we may sometimes notice differences. Possible reasons are: on one brand the trigrams need to be read from the inside outwards, on another from the outside inwards. Occasionally, a ba-gua might come off the production line with the screw in the wrong position.

### Later heaven sequence

The "Later Heaven sequence" is a dynamic ba-gua with continuous forces of interaction between the trigrams. It deals with daily life and matters of the here and now. Since the layout is based on the orientation of the seasons, there are different versions for the northern (clockwise rotation) and southern hemisphere (anti-clockwise rotation). See diagrams and a concise explanation in chapter "North-south considerations". For more detailed information, refer to the book "Feng Shui for the Southern Hemisphere" by the same author (published by Axiom Publishing).

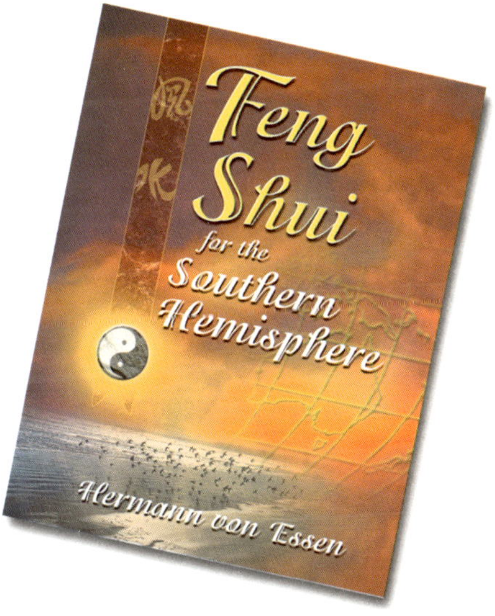

The layout and major attributes of the later heaven sequence are as follows:

| Chinese name | English name | Trigram | Magic square no. | Northern hemisphere | Southern hemisphere |
|---|---|---|---|---|---|
| **Li** | **Fire** | ☲ | 9 | South | North |
| **K'un** | **Earth** | ☷ | 2 | South-west | North-west |
| **Tui** | **Lake** | ☱ | 7 | West | West |
| **Chien** | **Heaven** | ☰ | 6 | North-west | South-west |
| **K'an** | **Water** | ☵ | 1 | North | South |
| **Ken** | **Mountain** | ☶ | 8 | North-east | South-east |
| **Chen** | **Thunder** | ☳ | 3 | East | East |
| **Sun** | **Wind** | ☴ | 4 | South-east | North-east |

The centre is not part of the ba-gua, but it exists nevertheless. Its properties are:

| | | | | | |
|---|---|---|---|---|---|
| **Tai ch'i** | **Self** | n.a. | 5 | Centre | Centre |

## Chinese name, English name and trigram

The meanings of these three columns have been explained in the chapter "Trigrams".

## Magic square numbers

"Lo-shu" numbers, originating from the tortoise shell (Chinese magic square), have been allocated to the trigrams as shown above. Logically, the highest number (9) associates with the highest level of energy: summer and fire (south in the northern hemisphere and north in the southern hemisphere). The lowest number (1) associates with the lowest level of energy: winter and water (north in the northern hemisphere and south in the southern hemisphere).

| energy | season | time of the day | family member | colour | life enhancing area |
|---|---|---|---|---|---|
| fire | summer | noon | middle daughter | red | fame reputation |
| big earth | late summer | afternoon | mother | brown yellow | relationships physical health |
| small metal | autumn | dusk | youngest daughter | white metal | communication recreation |
| big metal | early winter | evening | father | white metal | commerce helpful People |
| water | winter | midnight | middle son | blue black | career life path |
| small earth | late winter | early morning | youngest son | brown yellow | study, craft, skills, self-development |
| big wood | spring | dawn | eldest son | green | family, children, ancestors |
| small wood | early summer | morning | eldest daughter | green | prosperity wellbeing |
| earth | n.a. | n.a. | n.a. | brown yellow | emotional health |

## Northern and southern hemispheres

These columns position the trigrams in the northern and southern hemisphere versions of the later heaven sequence. The words north and south swap places between these columns, while east and west remain the same, expressing the "vertical flip" of hot and cold when we cross the equator.

## Energies and colours

The energies (and colours) are inseparable properties of the trigrams (see chapter: "Trigrams").

## Seasons

The allocated seasons demonstrate the different moods of the trigrams. We observe a clockwise rotation in the northern and an anticlockwise rotation in the southern hemisphere.

## The time of the day

The times rotate parallel to the seasons. Here, a full circle represents a day instead of a year.

## Family members

This is the traditional order allocating family members around the (usually round) dining table or determining their preferred sleeping positions in the house.

## Life-enhancing areas

The above table identifies the life-enhancing areas in a house, addressed in the next chapter.

A Buddha statue, a “helpful friend” to be positioned higher than ourselves.

## North-south considerations

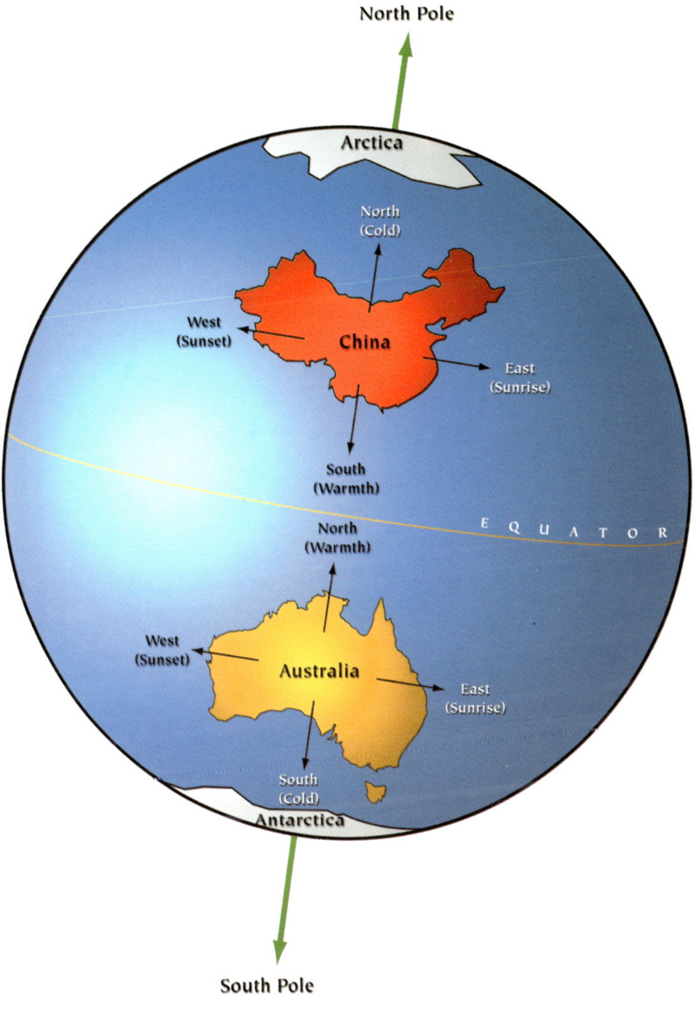

## Feng Shui

Looking at the ba-gua of the "Later heaven sequence", commonly used to identify life-enhancing areas in the house, we often find the following representations in Chinese notation and for the northern hemisphere: We observe that the forces between the trigrams rotate clockwise.

For simplicity, we have left out the in-between orientations: NW, NE, SW and SE, since they follow the same rules of adjustment and can be inserted at a later stage.

Note that the Chinese representation of the compass orientations is: north at the bottom, east on the left, south at the top and west on the right.

| | | | | |
|---|---|---|---|---|
| **North** | trigram "K'an" | water | cold | winter |
| **East** | trigram "Chen" | wood | sunrise | spring |
| **South** | trigram "Li" | fire | warmth | summer |
| **West** | trigram "Tui" | metal | sunset | autumn |

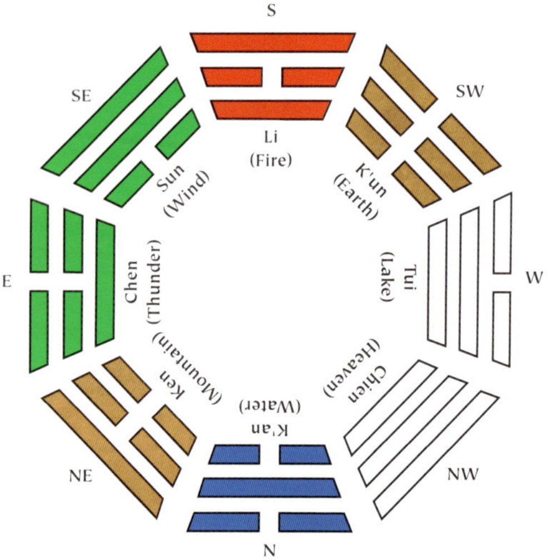


The authentic version of the later heaven sequence.

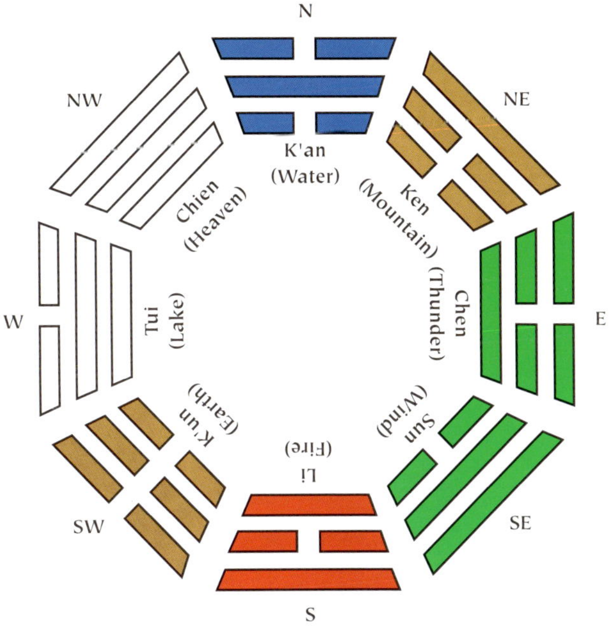


The western version of the northern hemisphere ba-gua.

Most Feng Shui books abide by this tradition, but some, published in Europe and the USA, have done us a favour and rotated the ba-gua 180˚, placing north at the top, east on the right, south at the bottom and west on the left. This is the **Western notation** for the **northern hemisphere**. It would be helpful if these books explained this, but most don't.

Although we now have obtained a readable ba-gua according to western standards, it is still for the **northern hemisphere**. In order to apply it to southern hemisphere conditions, we need to cross the equator. We start travelling in China with the north pole (cold) in the back and the equator (warmth) ahead of us. Once we cross the equator, we travel with the warmth in the back, heading for the south pole (cold). In other words: on the other side of the equator, **warmth** and **cold** or the elements **fire** and **water**, have swapped places. We now obtain the **Western notation** for the **southern hemisphere**:

| | | | | |
|---|---|---|---|---|
| **North** | trigram "Li" | fire | warmth | summer |
| **East** | trigram "Chen" | wood | sunrise | spring |
| **South** | trigram "K'an" | water | cold | winter |
| **West** | trigram "Tui" | metal | sunset | autumn |

We observe the forces between the trigrams rotate anti-clockwise.

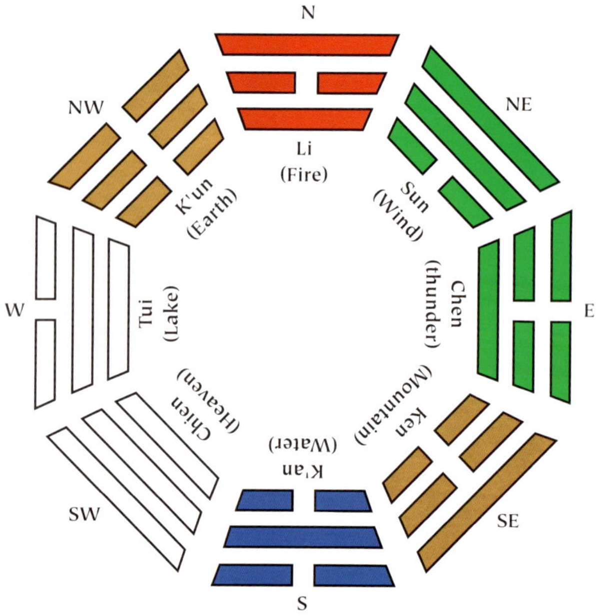


The western version of the southern hemisphere ba-gua.

**This is the only correct way to rework original Feng Shui orientations for southern hemisphere conditions**, automatically converting **clockwise vortex** rotation into **anti-clockwise**.

In a graphics computer, the adjustments of the original ba-gua can be performed easily by **180° rotation** followed by a **vertical flip**. This effect can be simulated by placing a traditional ba-gua face down on a glass coffee table and reading it from underneath.

The sum of both movements: **180° rotation** and **vertical flip** can be performed in a shortcut by simply **swapping left and right**. Thus, for the southern hemisphere: the relationships corner is far left (not far right as in the northern hemisphere) and the prosperity corner is far right (not far left). These locations are explained in the next chapter.

An active water feature, supporting a prosperity corner.

## Life Enhancing Areas

### Introduction

The life-enhancing areas are identified by the application of a "ch'i-distribution overlay" over the floor plan of the house. The spread is derived from the later heaven sequence ba-gua, with a different version for each hemisphere. Following the teachings of Feng Shui's " Black Hat school" we do not align the ba-gua with the compass but with the main entrance instead. Practically, the "k'an" side of the ba-gua (=water, and flow) is aligned with the wall containing the main entrance. This is a logical approach, since the trigram k'an expresses the flow of our career and life and the main entrance hosts the flow of ch'i.

### Steps to follow

1. Completion of the floor plan. If applicable, extend the floor plan on paper to obtain a complete rectangle, filling in the "missing corners". Additions, such as a garage, carport or pergola, need to be included if these are substantial, have at least a solid roof and are preferably constructed with the same building materials as the house and in the same style.
2. Selection of the ba-gua version. The version of the later heaven sequence ba-gua is selected depending on the hemisphere. Since climatic differences between the ba-guas are not distinct in tropical zones (Feng Shui was not developed in tropical regions), here we may choose the (traditional) northern hemisphere version as it is supported by a strong belief system.
3. Alignment of the ba-gua with the main entrance. We align the "k'an" side of the ba-gua with the main entrance, regardless whether it is left, centre or right in the wall or even receded. Our main entrance is the door we "arrive home through", usually also the main ch'i entry. It need not be the original front door if rarely used.
4. Extending the life-enhancing areas to the floor plan. Using the layout of the ba-gua, we assign all other life-enhancing areas to the four corners and the centres of the left, rear and right sides of the rectangle.

5. Addressing the life-enhancing areas. After identifying the areas in the house we can place some tokens in the appropriate spots. Here are some guidelines:

- Express purpose (try to express in a symbolic way our needs in that area of life).
- Use personal solutions (no two relationships corners are the same).
- Keep it simple (do not over-decorate the house).
- Identify all areas and ensure there is no clutter or rubbish stacked in these locations.

Find a weatherproof solution if an area falls outside the building. This can be a garden feature or even a beautiful wind chime if it is underneath a roof. It is unnecessary to see this situation as "a missing corner". It can be treated as an external area instead.

All life-enhancing areas can be identified in a small area (1 m. diameter). The "k'an" area is an exception. It is not a confined spot on the floor plan like the others. "K'an" representing our "career path" and also "life path" runs from the street along the usual route we follow to arrive home (including parking the car on the grounds, if applicable). Keep it inviting, harmonious, balanced, clean and tidy and unobstructed at all times (without the garbage bin in full sight). Our life path must be in good repair (no cracked concrete) and not represent "a rocky road". Finally, the "centre of the house" or "tai-ch'i" is found by drawing two diagonal lines through the corners of the extended rectangle (on paper).

## Conclusion

Create unique solutions when addressing life-enhancing areas. It is fun and it can change our life. These "physical affirmations" keep communicating with our subconscious on a daily basis. New ideas or changed insights may lead to updated or enhanced solutions.

## Life-enhancing areas (northern hemisphere)

This is the layout of life-enhancing areas in the northern hemisphere, after the k'an side has been aligned with the main entrance.

Example: the prosperity area is in the far left corner (of the rectangle) and the relationships area in the far right corner as seen from the main entrance.

| | | |
|---|---|---|
| **Sun**<br>Prosperity<br>Wealth | **Li**<br>Fame<br>Reputation | **K'un**<br>Relationships<br>Health |
| **Chen**<br>Family<br>Ancestors | **Tai-ch'i**<br>Self<br>Emotions | **Tui**<br>Creativity<br>Communication |
| **Ken**<br>Skills, Study<br>Self Development | **K'an**<br>Career<br>Life path | **Chien**<br>Commerce<br>Helpful people |
| Main entrance (anywhere in this wall) | | |

Although living plants and flowers can be beautiful and excellent energy enhancers, they need to look healthy (not droopy or dead).

An example of a relationships corner

## Life-enhancing areas (southern hemisphere)

This is the layout of life-enhancing areas in the southern hemisphere, after the k'an side has been aligned with the main entrance.

Example: the prosperity area is in the far right corner (of the rectangle) and the relationships area in the far left corner as seen from the main entrance.

| | | |
|---|---|---|
| **Kun**<br>Relationships<br>Wealth | **Li**<br>Fame<br>Reputation | **Sun**<br>Prosperity<br>Health |
| **Tui**<br>Creativity<br>Communication | **Tai-ch'i**<br>Self<br>Emotions | **Chen**<br>Family<br>Ancestors |
| **Chien**<br>Commerce<br>Helpful people | **K'an**<br>Career<br>Life path | **Ken**<br>Skills, Study<br>Self Development |
| Main entrance (anywhere in this wall) | | |

Introducing a waterfall softens the ch'i of a corner and can express "flow" in your prosperity corner at the same time.

## The five energies

### Introduction

The five energies (sometimes referred to as "elements") of Feng Shui have no relationship to the four energies used in astrology or the Tarot..

The five Feng Shui energies are:
earth – metal – water – wood – fire
Every landscape, building, object, person, business, etc. can be observed and analysed to assess which energies they represent.

### Representation of energies

Energies are represented by:

- Energy in its pure form
- Shapes
- Colours
- Birth year (of a person, a building or a business)

### Energy present in its pure form.

Example: the sea, a river, lake, creek, swimming pool, aquarium or even a bird bath represent "water". A flame of any kind represents "fire". An object made of real wood represents "wood", etc.

### Shapes

A landscape, building or object can also be classified by its most obvious shape. The characteristics of the five energies' shapes are:

Earth: flat, long, straight, square or rectangular (wider than tall)
Examples: a lawn, parking or any other flat area, straight street, floor, square or horizontal picture, etc.

Metal: round, oval, elliptic, dome-shaped
Examples: a tree with a round crown, dome shaped shrub, round clock, etc.

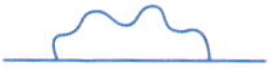

Water: waving, weaving, irregular, asymmetric
Examples: a winding road, garden path, border line, etc.

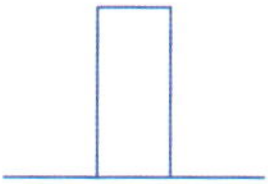

Wood: parallel rising vertical lines, column-shaped, rectangular (taller than wide)
Examples: a multi-storey building, door, vertical picture. Etc.

Fire: sharp, pointy, steep, arrow-shaped
Examples: a pine tree, conifer, cypress, cliff face, etc.

Balance between the five elements: brown and a flat surface for “earth”, round shrubs for “metal”, an irregular shaped and grey roof for “water”, a green lawn and vertical windows for “wood” and red bricks for “fire”.

### Colours are represented as follows:

Earth: brown, yellow, cream
Metal: white and metal colours, such as: gold, silver, bronze, copper, brass, pewter, nickel, chromium, aluminium, etc.
Water: black, blue
Wood: green
Fire: red

Orange, purple, pink, etc. combine two of the above colours and thus share two energies.

### Years of birth

(starting in the first week of February!) are represented as follows:

Earth: last digit 8 or 9
Metal: last digit 0 or 1
Water: last digit 2 or 3
Wood: last digit 4 or 5
Fire: last digit 6 or 7

The five energies at work in nature.

## Meaning of the five energies theory

After assessing the five energies, there are two strategies to follow:

- Promote harmonious combinations of neighbouring energies, using the "Creative cycle". Avoid interfering combinations by rearranging objects or by placing a "mediator" in between.
- Achieve an equilibrium (equal representation) between all five energies within a certain territory.

## Neighbouring energies

Usually, the five Feng Shui energies are presented as:
earth – metal – water – wood – fire.
This order is called the "creative cycle", with the following reasoning:

- From the minerals of the earth we create metal
- From the solid state of metal we create the liquid state (symbolising water) by heating
- With help from the water we grow wood
- With wood we feed a fire
- From the ashes of the fire we recycle earth

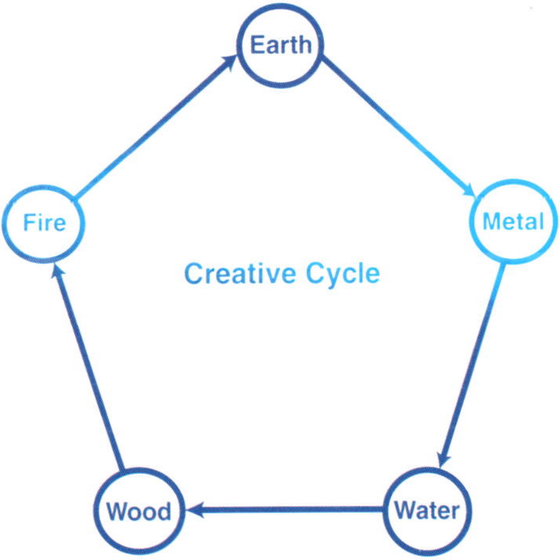

We can also place the energies in the order:
earth – water – fire – metal – wood

This is called the destructive, or more pleasantly, the control cycle, with the following reasoning:

- Earth muddles water
- Water douses a fire
- Fire melts metal
- Metal chops up wood
- Wood depletes the earth

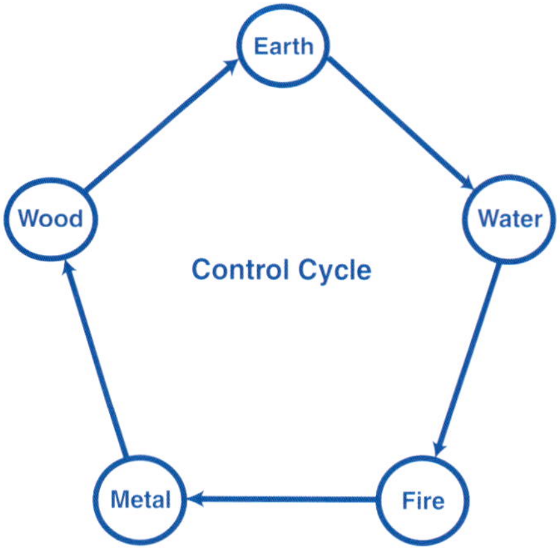


These are the two most important cycles, although two more exist. From these cycles we can learn how to resolve a clash between, for instance, "water" and "fire": we select a "wood" energy to place in between. (A mediator between two people or an object between two other objects).

### Creating equal representation

Achieve an equilibrium between the five energies in order to balance any particular territory. This can be a room, house, view from a particular window, garden, property, street, town, etc. A practical method includes the following steps:

One: Define the territory to be assessed.

Two: Assess the energies of every item observed within this territory. Several items may represent more than one energy. For example, a red door represents "wood" (by shape) and "fire" (by colour). A practical way is to write an inventory list with five energy columns and rate the representations of energies of every item, say on a scale of 1 – 10.

Three: Add up the five columns. There is a good balance if the sums are in the same range. Work needs to be done if some energies are over-dominant or under-represented,.

Four: Balance serious differences. Either reduce some of the over-dominant energies or add to the representation of weaker ones. Every case is different and careful observation, thought and inventiveness leads to the best solution.

It is obvious that a house on the beach is under influence of an "over-water" environment. Since it is not possible to reduce the presence of water, the other energies need to be added in substantial quantities.

## Conclusion

If a street, garden, house or room intuitively "feels good", inviting or even cosy, there is usually a reasonable balance between the five energies. An energies assessment will confirm this. When a place feels uninviting and unpleasant on entering, there is almost invariably an imbalance between the energies and an assessment can help pinpoint the problem areas.

Balance of the five elements applied to food presentation.

## The Celestial Animals

### Introduction

Feng Shui pays specific attention to our immediate environment, as it influences our health, wealth and well-being. This topic is called "the Celestial animals" theory. Although there are five celestial animals, they are sometimes presented as four, leaving out the centre (our point of observation). The five animals are:

- The black tortoise (energy "water")

- The red phoenix (energy "fire")

- The green dragon (energy "wood")

- The white tiger (energy "metal")

- The brown snake (energy "earth")

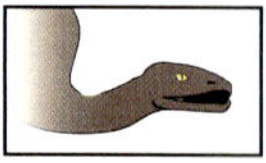

### The black tortoise

The black tortoise is the highest surrounding elevation, offering protection and shelter. In moderate climates (such as China and the southern half of Australia), the black tortoise is positioned to protect us from the prevailing cold and wet weather. In the northern hemisphere, this is from the north, in the southern hemisphere from the south.
In the hills, the black tortoise is the highest elevation of the sloping land. On the suburban plains, it is the highest neighbouring building or a group of large trees and in open farm land, it is a wind shield of substantial trees or a large shed. Inside a room, the black tortoise is a solid wall without doors or windows, offering "protection in the back" above the headboard of the bed or behind seating.

The black tortoise associates with: protection, the energy "water', cold, winter, midnight, darkness and the colours black or blue.

Balanced, but lacking a control position.
The sofa is not backed by a "black tortoise".

## The red phoenix

The red phoenix is the lowest surrounding elevation, offering unobstructed views and vision. It offers openness towards light and warmth. In the northern hemisphere it has a southerly aspect, in the southern hemisphere a northerly aspect.

In the hills, the red phoenix represents the lowest elevation of the sloping land and the direction of the views. On the suburban plains, it represents some distance into an obstruction-free garden, street or reserve and in open farm land, it offers views over the fields. If the red phoenix has some elevation at all, it needs to be restricted to a low flower bed or very low shrubs.

The red phoenix associates with: vision, energy "fire", warmth, summer, light and the colour red.

A post, blocking the "red phoenix" of this window.

### The green dragon

The green dragon has a medium elevation and is positioned preferably in the east. Thus: in the northern hemisphere it is on our left (looking southwards with the black tortoise in the back) and in the southern hemisphere it is on our right side (looking northwards with the black tortoise in the back). The green dragon can be slightly higher or equal in height to our own house. It can be represented by the slope of the land, a neighbouring building or group of medium sized trees.

The green dragon associates with: new life and ch'i, the energy "wood", sunrise, spring, dawn and the colour green.

### The white tiger

The white tiger is always opposite the dragon and therefore located in the west. The dragon and tiger form a pair and keep each other in balance (yin & yang). They are often depicted as a pair on a Chinese plate, vase or scarf. The white tiger is slightly lower and must never dominate the green dragon. It can be represented by the slope of the land, a neighbouring building or group of medium sized trees.

The white tiger associates with: strength and vigilance (let it not turn against you by allowing it to be over-proportioned), energy "metal", sunset, autumn, dusk and the colour white or metallic.

## The brown snake

The brown snake is our own point of observation: the house relating to its environment or the bed or seating relating to the room and other furniture. It associates with: the centre, energy "earth", neutrality and the colour brown.

## Application areas

The application areas of the celestial animals are manifold.

- Inside the house, it illustrates the "control position", making us feel good and at ease (see next chapter). There are many variations depending on the type of room assessed.
- In hills areas, it illustrates a good block of land has the lowest elevation and views towards the equator. Land that is "the wrong way around" often has a water problem. The sun never shines directly onto the land. Therefore it never dries completely and a house may suffer from salt damp, mildew, lack of ch'i, wood rot, detrimental energies from moving underground water underneath a bedroom, etc. In the afternoon, it will be early in shadow. The total package can have a depressing effect on the occupants.
- In suburban areas, it illustrates a good property must not be built-out by a close neighbouring house, a high fence or an uncontrollable group of large trees on the side facing the equator.

Seeking the only control position at this table.

## Control Position

### Introduction

Feng Shui describes our "control position" as the position within a certain territory in which we are fully in control of our environment. This can apply to a property, lounge, bedroom, kitchen, office, reception, etc. Being in a control position gives us confidence and peace of mind at all times. We feel better, perform better and reduce our stresses, all of which have a positive effect on our health.

### The celestial animals at work

The essentials of a control position are a practical derivative of the "celestial animals" theory:

- The "black tortoise", representing the highest elevation which surrounds us and offering "protection" and "security" behind us.
- The "red phoenix", representing the lowest elevation which surrounds us and offering "view" and "vision" in front of us.

The "green dragon" and "white tiger" are medium height objects to our right and left sides, but they are less important for the control position. The Tortoise and Phoenix are the most important aspects describing the control position.

### Control position principles

Firstly, we need perfect protection behind us. This applies to the headboard of a bed or the back of any chair or sofa. The easiest representation of a black tortoise is a solid wall. In this position, we will never be caught by surprise from the back. Even if we know who else is in the house, subconsciously it causes unrest and stress to sit with our back exposed to a door, passage or even a window.

Secondly, we need some free space in front of us. If our red phoenix is blocked, our vision will not reach far and we will be limited to achieving short-term goals only. Thus, Feng Shui recommends we avoid placing a desk facing the wall. To be in control, our red phoenix must contain all doors, passages and windows, even if we can see them only in our peripheral vision. In this position, we cannot be surprised.

## The bedroom

Here is an example of a good bedroom layout.

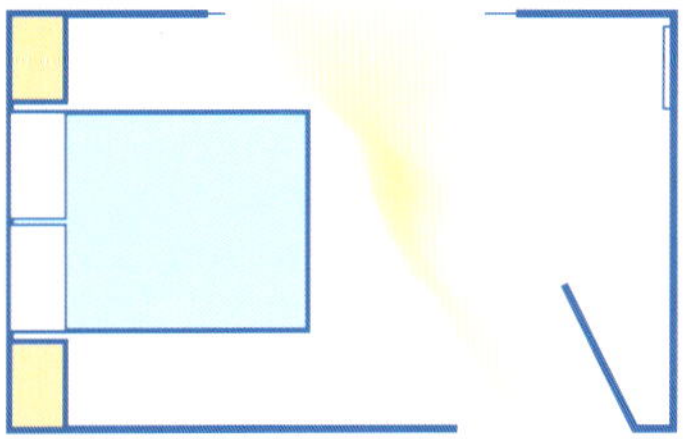

We also avoid placing the bed in the ch'i-draught invariably occurring between the door and window.

## The office

Here is an example of a good office layout.

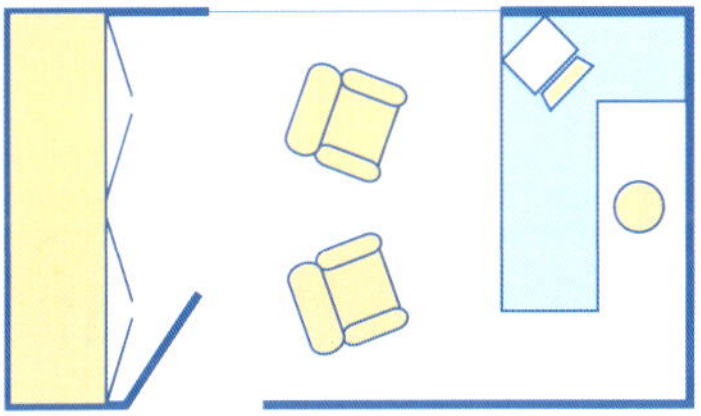

When laying out an office, people often tend to place desks against walls and then arrange the remaining furniture. It is more beneficial for the office staff to apply the Feng Shui method: Position the chairs first, backed by solid walls and facing doors and windows. Next, place the desks in front of the chairs. Computer monitors are preferably positioned on the window side of the desk and at least 1.2 m distance from the operator. Also, when looking up from the papers of a desk, it is beneficial for the eyes to temporarily focus on infinity by looking through a window, preferably onto natural surroundings. In typical Feng Shui cities like Hong Kong and Singapore, beliefs state positioning the general manager's desk facing a wall is a guaranteed recipe for bankruptcy.

## Other applications of the control position

The control position applies to many areas of our life. It is important to analyse those areas where we spend most of our time and to abide by the control position principles in those locations. Once we are familiar with the essence of the control position, we automatically apply this to places where we spend only a short period of time and we find the best available seat in a tram, bus or train, restaurant or theatre.

## The student's or teenager's room

The student's or teenager's room is an area often overlooked and which can combine the functions of a bedroom, sitting room and study. When the positioning of a bed, wardrobe, small desk with chair, set of bookshelves and easy chair is determined along the principles of the control position, it offers the student a better chance in life and better study results.

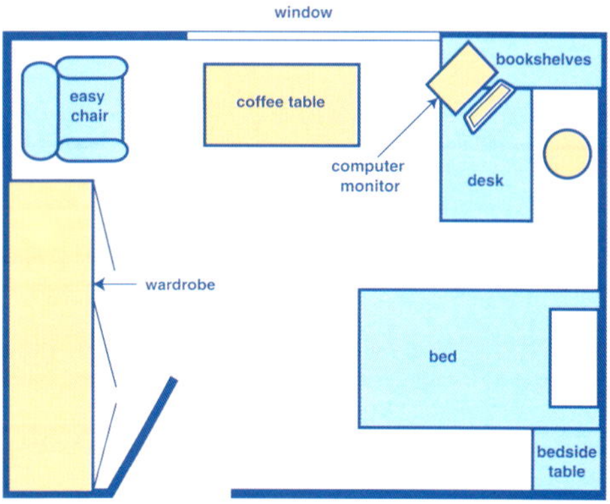


Here is an illustration of a good student's room. Note the positioning of a computer monitor (if one is required). The distance between the screen and the body is at least 1.2 meters.

## Shaping a Healthy House

### Environmental Energies can affect our Health

So far, we have explored various areas of Feng Shui relating to the continuous energy exchange between ourselves and our home. Besides a well-maintained house with a balanced floor plan, situated in a peaceful location, it is important to decorate it with harmonious furnishings and balanced colours. A good ch'i-flow in a clutter-free household, with a fresh bouquet of flowers on the table, sets the stage for a successful and healthy life.

However, Feng Shui offers us only part of the required wisdom. Just as important is the other part, related to "Environmental Energies". These can be man-made or natural.

### Man-made environmental energies

Man-made energies mostly consist of 50 Hz EMR (electro-magnetic radiation) and MWR (microwave radiation).

- External sources. The most common sources of EMR are powerlines (overhead and underground) and power transformers. MWR is emitted by mobile phone towers, communication transmitters and radar stations. The exposure and dangers depend on the strength of the source and the distance from our house. Energy levels can be verified with reliable measuring equipment. Although some deflecting devices can be designed and installed to reduce the effects of radiation, it would be more prudent to carry out a short pre-purchase analysis to identify local energies, prior to signing a contract for a new property.
- Internal sources. With some awareness, we can observe safe minimum distances from EMR-sources in the house, such as: the meter box, TV, computer monitor, fridge, microwave oven, clock radio, fax machine, fluoro lights, transformers to halogen lights, touch-sense lamp, power supplies to a mobile phone charger, answering machine, etc. Keep these devices out of the bedroom in the first place and avoid steel or iron components in the bed frame. Even the coils in spring coil mattresses work like

little antennas and rebroadcast EMR. Consider sleeping on a futon (made of cotton and wool) instead. A simple tip: trade in electric blankets for hot water bottles.

In a high level EMR environment, with many EMR sources around us, internally or externally, the presence of iron and steel is an additional disadvantage. Steel beams, used in the construction of a house, can relay EMR from a distant power transformer into the house. Similar conduct can be expected from steel window and door frames, steel gutters, galvanised iron water pipes, steel roof or wall sheeting and to a greater extent: steel frame houses.

An unsuitable neighbour.

## Natural environmental energies

Natural energies are related to the earth and cosmos and they vary with the location of a property. There is a wide variety of influences possible, such as:

- Geopathic stress from earth fault lines (causing stress and tension)
- Geomagnetic positive lines (healing certain parts of the body)
- Geomagnetic negative lines(damaging certain parts of the body)
- Lines of the Hartmann grid (causing insomnia and unrest)
- Lines of the Curry grid (contributing to ME, cancer and arthritis)

- Radiation from underground water movement (contributing to cancer)
- Positive ley-lines (mind stimulating)
- Negative ley lines (mind depressing)
- Microwave corridors (may contribute to Alzheimer's disease)
- Gamma radiation and Radon gas (contributing to cancer)

An energy analysis can identify and map the relevant influences on a property. Besides the use of some technical instruments, the art of dowsing is the major tool used in such analyses. The most important task is to ensure bed positions are "clean".

The presence of (unexplainable and often incurable) illnesses and medical conditions can be an indication that a house and its occupants are being affected. In Germany, the term "cancer house" and even "cancer street" is known and understood.

Do not build a house here, as these trees suffer from geopathic stress

The formation of mountains often concurs with earth fault-lines. In several mountainous regions of Germany and Austria, a geomancer's report, stating that the land is free of geopathic stress, is required before a building permit can be issued. Even in countries without such legislation, an environmental energies analysis, with optional Feng Shui assessment, is usually a good investment in our health and prosperity.

## Follow up

### Opening Feng Shui awareness

There is much more to Feng Shui than could possibly be covered in this book. Additionally to practical guidance it invites the reader to embark on a Feng Shui journey of continued discovery. The keys are conscious observation and expanded perception. This is how Feng Shui developed over many centuries, observing correlations between aspects of human life and environment.

### Self-scrutiny

A Feng Shui consultant analysing a house observes the situation with a fresh and unbiased view, whereas occupants accustomed to their environment may not notice rather obvious areas of potential improvements, leaving them unattended for years.

Involvement with Feng Shui automatically activates a positive self-scrutiny avoiding this. An example: any broken item needs repair or replacement, preferably not next week or next year but right now! Ignoring this affects the quality of our environment and thus the quality of our life.

### Awareness of beauty and clutter

Displaying beautiful art, ornaments or furniture improves ambiance and sheng-ch'i, whereas clutter manifests staleness by introducing sha- and si-ch'i, stagnating our life. Excess clutter has a tendency to multiply, becoming a powerful opponent difficult to conquer.

A household, run on the above principles usually "looks good", "feels good" and has "good Feng Shui". We feel happy, peaceful and in harmony with our environment and co-occupants. As a result, we are more "in control" of our lives.

### A basic Feng Shui principle

your **house** reflects your life

your **life** reflects your house

**These are inseparable!**

Improving the quality of life means: paying attention to the quality of the house and its environment (this principle applies also to our car or business).

### Feng Shui study

Study takes time as there is much more involved than simply absorbing theory. Methods are:

- Private study with a proficient Feng Shui Master (traditional method).
- Attending courses and workshops (more accessible, present method).
- Taking correspondence courses (easy introduction).
- Individual study by reading Feng Shui books (often confusing).

There are many Feng Shui books on the market. Most focus on "authentic" Feng Shui, excellent for basic understanding and application in the northern hemisphere but usually impractical for application in the southern hemisphere.